GLORY OF THE WOODS

A POETIC EXPERIENCE

SHAFIKA FATHIMA

ISBN 979-888521680-7

God Almighty

(Who made it all possible!)

Contents

Contents

Foreword

Glory of the Woods is a collection of poems celebrating the beauty of the forest. Every natural aspect has deep mysteries that amaze us. It has wisdom beyond measure from which we learn every day. It teaches us ways to live life and is one of our earliest scholars. This book celebrates the jungle aspects of nature where living and non-living being has a lot to offer. The poems bring out the aesthetic beauty of the forests in different ways. Peculiar and totally amazing beings from all over the world have been written about. The beauty of the forests is as varied and deep as the oceans. The book covers the most minimum of the astounding forests. The motive is to give you a poetic experience of a stroll through the forest. So buckle up to begin the jungle safari! Happy Reading!

Acknowledgements

I would love to thank the following people for being a part of the book. Firstly, my parents whose constant support I experienced throughout this journey. I also thank my extended family for having both inspired and supported me with or without knowledge. My exclusive set of friends whose support I was very lucky to have during this time. You believed in my work more than I did, continued to encourage me and your unwavering support was default at all times. I am very grateful for that! I would also like to thank my teachers and mentors who helped reach here, in particular the teachers of St.Joseph's Convent, Coonoor. I thank the Notion Press team for this wonderful opportunity and am very delighted that I got to work with you. I also thank all my well-wishers and ask for your continued support. I also would like to thank the members of the writing community who take the time to read the works of others apart from their own. Your words of appreciation help every other writer, me in particular to keep going!

God Almighty

Giving is His nature, the only constant among the changinG

Obedience Is His liking, abiding to Him is what I'll always dO

Divine are His creations – which if counted can never enD

Amazing is His Wisdom, deeper than any ocean or seA

Loving me beyond my mother, He sure is pure and eternaL

Miracles are His making, the universe is His kingdoM

Inescapable is His wrath, beyond any protection or alibI

Greatness and grandeur are not enough acclaiminG

Hidden in every atom, His testimonials of power and strengtH

Trusting You is what I'll always do, without which I can't persisT

You Lord, are truly my beginning and my peripherY

POETIC EXPERIENCE

1. The Forest

• 3 •

In the Kingdom of Earth its the princess,
A land where no humans roam.
Slender trees casting a delightful darkness
Wildlife call it their home,
It surely is distinct than the rest

The Zebra with its phenomenal stripes,

The giraffe with its neck held high,
Even the crocodile's ruthless fights;
Is all a feast to the eye!

• 4 •

The wind whispering a rhythm of its own
The distant roar of a tiger
A cuckoo's lonely mourn
Hand in hand with the gushing water

The mist thickening, as white as snow
The clouds escorting the rain so as to nurture – Besides
Revealing the concealed glow – of that
Which is the best quintessence of Nature!

2. The Great Banyan

She lived near the forest
In a tiny hut with her kin.
Every day with her pop, went she, into the woods
A five year old skipping along side.
That day was like no other
Except, she saw tree, a solitary one!
The trunk of an elephant's size,
Beside which she was a tiny ant.
With hanging roots & heavy branches – which
She thought were separate trees.
Gaping, she said, "Pop, what's this?"
"Its the Great Banyan my kid
The king of trees." said he.
Pointing around 10 meters he cried,
"Can you believe? That's the next tree!
Shoots from nothing n another man's land,
To build its kingdom, a canopy by its own.
Hence called the strangler's fig.
Aided by wasps, it grows, providing protection,
To animals & birds sp they can rest"
Looking up she thought
"Every leaf has a story to tell,
Oh, I hear the laughter & the cheers!"

Her heart swelled with pride,
"The Great Banyan" she breathed.

3. The squeaky squirrel

Scuttling through the ground
In the stillness of the forest
Searching food, going round and round
Looking for a nest
In the trees, grass or rubble
Yes, its the squirrel.

In the stillness of the forest
During day and night
With a constant scurrying tumult
Tree to tree, left and right
Jumping and zigzagging through fallen leaves
Dodging predators and hiding in cleavages.

Searching food, going round and round
Insects and tiny birds, but mostly nuts – and
Burying them in holes, for later, to be found
After inspecting, for scratches & cuts
Prominent is the shake test, for the seed.
Without which the nut's a weed.

Looking for a nest
In pairs or alone, for kids

Giving its best
A secure place, well protected, avoiding risks
Away from sunlight, as young ones are blind,
Tender care is how, the finest sight, they find!

In the trees, grass or rubble,
Their storage is an interesting story,
Finding the right nuts they scuttle
To locate a spot to bury.
Some even have storage categories
Others might lose the spot from their memories.

Yes, its the squirrel
The tiny little rodent
As amazing as the turtle
Very witty and prudent
Having a 300 of its kind
They grow more trees than all of mankind!

4. Soil

The cashew always wondered
Mmm...Mmm...Mmm...
What lay underneath the soil, firm grounded?
Crunch...crunch...crunch...
Only when planted inside deep
Dig...dig...dig...
It discovered an enormous world in a single peep
Wow, wow, wow!
Earthworms grunting, Ants Singing;
Titch...titch...titch...
Nitrogen and CO2 bubbling
Bloop, bloop, bloop
Its fellow seeds, at him beamed,
Smile, Smile, Smile...
"The soil by itself is a lovely flower blossomed"
Bloom, Bloom, Bloom!

5. Arjuna

The Arjuna with its yellow flower, whose
Every part has medicinal power!
The bark, powdered heals the heart,
And it surely has no counterpart.

The Arjuna with its woody fruit
That heals wounds within a swift
With eaves that are greenish brown
Adorning the tree like a lavish crown!

Native to the Indian subcontinent
The Arjuna is certainly magnificent!

6. Humming Bird

Its a charming tiny bird
Almost smallest
It has a beak
Like a syringe.

With over 350 different kinds
From the smallest bee
To the giant
They range alot.

Feeding on insects & nectar
And mostly rests
To save power
When food is scarce

Velvety compact with twigs as
The nest, just like
It, very small
For bean-like eggs.

With spongy floors & elastic walls
So to expand
As the young grows,
Such convenience!

Its wings flapping makes the eyes blur
And producing
The humming sound
And thus it's name

Humming bird is flabbergasting
Admired by not
Just bird lovers
But every man!

7. The Deer

Galloping and leaping,
The sound of hooves...
Past meadows and bushes
Running from lions and wolves...

In herds among grasslands
Mother and fawn in sins of mellow,
In constant danger from every predator,
Let alone, the hunter's arrow...

Yet the deer doesn't stop existing
Nor does it stop running...
Cause it finds joy in small moments
And likes giving the best at all times...
Maybe, we too need to be a deer,
Sometimes...

8. Caves

A sandy floor with a rocky roof – where
The hunter rests with his horse & its hoof
They are small as well as huge – a place for
Bats & lions to take refuge
Its where the early humans lived
And left legacies on the walls, scribbled.
Excavators find it impelling – to
Unearth history & for exploring
Its a dwelling that nature gave- yes
It is the cave!

9. Tyger

I'm an intriguing cat, always on guard,
You'd rather not have me in your backyard.
Striped not just fur but the skin,
I live solitary away from my kin.
I'm mightier than the lion and
Its no big deal to kill a bison.

I might have man eater cousins
So you wanna mess with me? Think in dozens!
You thinkin' of escaping my grasp?
Dude, even my tongue is razor-sharp!
I prefer hunting in ambush at night,
Six times better than yours is my eye sight.
I can swim even in the sea,
So the water can't stop me.
Also, I don't need medicine for bruises
My saliva has antiseptic uses.
Camouflage strategy – from my prey's back, I arise
Cause I love taking them by surprise!
I know what you're wondering,
That's right, I am amazing!

10. Spidery Thoughts...

Cobble webs, spooky legs...
Giant hairy ones
Tiny invisible ones
The spiders...
I sat under a tree watching one,
Happened to be its time of perseverance,
Like Alexander's story of emergence,
It kept trying to build its web...
It's web...
Intriguing thought – why does it build it?
Why can't it, like other insects, hunt?
No wings, yeah...
But blssed with eight legsAnd swift movements too!
Then it hit me,
The web was a sign of strength
A disguised weapon
The spider doesn't go after its demand,
It attracts it, more like a beckon;
Thus the web's a sign of power
Of authority,
Though it is more fragile
Than a flower...

11. Holly Oak

I lived in the countryside
All my childhood
My pa grazed sheep in the pastures, wide.
For a livelihood.
And me, always by his side.

A giant oak tree standing in the middle
Is where we rest, in its shade,
And where I learnt the fiddle
Until the sun into the clouds, will fade.
Or in case of a drizzle.

At times, I went there alone
And laid down under the oak – cause
I didn't want it being on its own
When a squirrel or an occasional duck
Would wander by to get an acorn.

As a child I had no friends,
But a million leaves for company
The oak's canopy would over me, bend,
Instilling a comforting harmony,
A happiness that never end!

12. The buzzing mystery

The bear cub walked in solitude
An amateur, his eyes widened
Seeing the honey comb so ripened,
Worker, drone and Queen
All bustling, yet serene...

The cub stood wonder struck,
A unison that inspired
A beauty to be admired
Toiling for days, contributing in multiple ways,
They function with one mind,
A bond so well refined...

The cub wondered,
"How can such unison exist?
In a world where,
Even tracing one's own writing
Is gnarly"
Well my friend, that sure is a mystery!

13. Tailor Bird

A lone bird with a glow
And a needle like beak
It sure does in our minds blow
With its stitching skills
Infamous for the nest it does grow
Using just leaves and cotton
Tiny yet Nature's best tailor though
With perseverance at its peak
Calm and composed with work so slow...

All that out of love& care
For young ones that are to hatch
A lot of sufferings she does bare
To ensure the tiny ones' protection
Fighting against anything it can scare
Saving the kids from threats
Once grown they go elsewhere
The fact doesn't let her detach
Though short lived she wishes for their welfare
With such inspiring impressions
Nature teaches us her lessons.

14. Butterfly

Beauty and hope
Beauty and spring
Spring appears
Spring's the wing
Wings they are
Wings so elegant

Elegant fluttering

Elegantly smooth & slow

Slow revamp

Slow & Steady

Steady progress

Steady success

Success so ideal

Success of the woods

The woods, where it prevails

The woods also the city

City folks are happy, oh yeah!

City & the woods it does add colour

Colour of the wings, oh my!

Colours splashed with radiance

Radiance of patience

Radiance of summer

Summer & spring like bread n butter

Summer's pal, spring is round the corner

Corner and quiet

Corner and Mystique

Mystical Elegance

Mystically ravishing all!

15. The River

The calf's first time to the river,
Amazed her beyond measure.
Guided by her mother's trunk,
She stepped inside from the bank.
Tiny fishes tickled her legs; without fear
Gushing water sang in her ears...
Looking at where the flow bended;
She wondered if the river ever ended,
Quenching the thirst of all living being
Where they can all drink to their stomach's filling!

16. Crocodile Tales

I gaze at my image in the water
The river I live in
I gaze at myself, and I see...
Spines...Ruthlessness...
I've never seen dad do that,
He's all confidence,
Of course, with mighty jaws as his,
You don't fight for independence!
Stealth's the strategy for survival
Among our tribe,
Ain't I supposed to feel sorry?
I daren't ask dad thugh!
My self-discrimination
Always led to hesitation
And I was dad's unworthy heir,
But I couldn't,
Couldn't change any of it...
Until...
I overheard the crow,
Talking to her chick.
"Don't give a thought of regret
Don't let yourself forget
You are a black beauty

No being can do what you can,
Even if they try and risk
They can't get even close,
So do the best you,
And amaze your spectators"
Wow! She was right!
I looked at me in the water,
That day, and whispered,
Do the best you...

17. The Umbrella Bird

The Black Egert
Is discrete among the
Fish-eating birds.

With yellow feet and
Black feathers it
Turns into an umbrella

Oh yes, its
A hunting strategy to
Fool the fish.

They do come for
Shade unaware of
The predator's beak

Living in flocks of
Many, hard to spot
One, on its own.

With yellow feet & black
Feathers the Egret is
An umbrella bird...

18. Mr. Green

Croak...Croak...

Clop...

The moon peered down

Flickering in pursuit of the sound's source

Was it the rock, on the soil very brown?

Leaning closer she noticed the green fellow

He reminded her of the mellow.
Talk of green and lush,
Here he is, frondescence plush.
The moon watched with attention, undivided
As he croaked and leapt,
Swam and hopped
Catching insects unseen...
A beauty of the night so serene
She adored the little frog
As dawn crept in...
She whispered,
"Oh! Croakery Fellow,
You're a trademark...
Until tomorrow, Mr.Green!"

19. The Crane

As she flapped to take off
I flew away from her...
Strange
I always fly with her,
I flew...flew down...
Coming to rest on the lushly grass.
And I watched as the white crane,
My mother flew past the horizon,
I, the fallen feather ain't gonna forget her,
She is a beauty,
An epitome,
I'm oblivious of the eco system
But she is an Oracle
For action so propitious,
That proverbs and scriptures
Speak of her...
My mother, the crane...

20. Fascinating Rhino

Not noticed is, the fascinating rhino
Just another animal? Why, No!
With surprising features
They are wonderful creatures.
Can't jump like other mammals
But can charge in any battles.
Despite being plant-eaters
Feared by all predators.
The only rival is man,
Hunted for their horn.
Poor eyesight made up with sense of smell,
The oxpeckers and them get along well.
Idols of calm & quiet, although
When provoked they're a deadly foe!

21. The Bluebell

Its the precursor of the summer
With sweet fragrance & an alluring gaze.
The English's favourite flower.

Adorning the woody lands
Enlightening the spring's end
It's the precursor of the summer.

A blue-violet bell, as in the name
Aided by ants, holding for bees, its nectar.
With sweet fragrance & an alluring gaze.

The beauty might even cure cancer
Its called the flower of fairies
The English's favourite flower!

22. Grasshopper

A pleasant green in a grassy meadow
Never fails to startle us, the hopper
With its reflex caper
Chirp Chirp Chirp
Chirp Chirp Chirp
In whose absence, the Pasteur becomes patchy though...

Eafy green to a woody brown
Distinguished by the sonic rhythm
That only a few can fathom
Those whom it enthrals;
Those whom it enthrals,
The hopper watchers in town!

Prey to a huge animal prism
Chew gut is its defence mechanism
Protein shakes of the foresters
Enemies of the farmers
A commonly exclusive bliss
The Grasshopper sure is!

23. The Light

Not a single day thou hath forgotten
To warm the heart of thy grounds
Relieving the frost bitten
Raising the spirits of all that mourns

Thee it is that wakes all life- aye
An intimation of dawn.
The cue for predators to begin th'r strife
Killing the deer or its fawn.

Oh! How sweet is the plant's love towards thee.
Not mindeth to twist or revolve
Every shrub even the tree – for
Thy ardeth crucial, for them to evolve.

Aiding the distressed to prosper
Hope & Wisdom is thy metaphor!

24. Datura Metal

A lovely white trumpet just like bluebell
The petals as though woven together
Commonly named as the devil's weed & Hell's bell,
As every chunk is so fatal, rather!
Yellow, red, violet are all its brother,
Differing in the colour of flower.

Its called the solanaceaes' power
Contrasting green leaves and thorn apple fruit
Does make the one who, consumes sick and sour
A beauty with poison in its boot!

25. Apes

Leaps and Chatters
Tails and limbs
Branches and trees
Yes its the Apes!
From cuddly little ones
To giant Gorillas
Visitors to our habitats
Giving us glimpses of wild lives...
Epics of social life
Advisors of the forest- Quiet wise
We humans got to stay cautious – else
We might just lose our kingdom to the Apes!

26. The Ungurahua

Abundant in the Amazon
A member of the palms
Slender & tall like a pine
Flourishing in the rain

The yellow floret giving rise to
With a striking colour, the fruit
Discovered by the women tribes
Its oil nourishes the hair's roots

Hidden beauty
Of the tree community
The Ungurahua
Is in dubiously Whoa!

27. Koala

You must've heard of the koala
Holla!
Its a bear like marsupial with fur
Her

Carrying the baby in a pouch
Ouch!
The claws are pointed!
Ted
Is what for its mistaken
Waken
In the Australian forests
Rests
For 22 hours a day
A
Tree branch is its home
Home!

28. Mynah

Typical bird it is
Often unnoticed like the crow
Exclusive o the peninsular region
No its not the sparrow
Unappreciated beauty – called plain
Why! I've never seen a better combination
Of black, white & yellow
The glorious creation!
As any other scholar (of the wild)
With a teaching so precise
To strive during change
And be ever willing to mould and mobilize...

29. The Wind

It isn't revealed to the eye sight
Its presence is vital to exist
Without which life would become a constant fight

Whooshing through the trees amid the silent night
Where the last of autumn leaves persist
Dropping them down like a feather, gentle & light

It snuffs out a fire burning bright
The blaze of anger and conflict – thus
Reviving peace; making enemies polite.

Odourless or colourless, be it might
A huge family it does consist – where in
Every member is bonded tight.

Ranging through, when anger is at its height
Blood-curdling though, I should admit
Scathing the land left and right.

Gentle or hoarse based on requisite
Harmony and Joy is what it subsists
The wind does have an essence of upright!

Embarking on us an excellent morale!

30. A pigeon's story

It was a fortnight
Since autumn began
When I glimpsed day light
Wriggled out of the shell as much as i can
And kept my eyes closed tight
For a two day span

Mother sheltered me all day
Dad put food in my beak
It was a nest, where we stay
A rock's crevice pn a hill's peak
I could watch trees sway,
From my corner if I peek

After a week or so
I had rough little feathers
They didn't have the glow
Like my mother's
I was patient though
Wanting to be beautiful than my brothers

I loved being a chick
Resting all the time

With food brought so quick
At the correct chime
Dad warned me of threats that lurk
Like predators to whom we're food very prime

Growing up with dad & mother
I heard a lot of stories
About how we can self-recognize in a mirror
About the urban cities
To which many of us moved nearer
Further away from the woods' territories

At long last the day dawned
Chirping we marched to the edge
To take off to the beyond
The instant our wings flapped, its the pledge
Whether we are striving or doomed,
Its on our own that we fledge...

31. Tulsi

• 45 •

There persists a wondrous medicine leaf

From cold to cancer it cures all

Its native to India,

Exists for centuries

Found & Used by chiefs in

Ayurveda

It is the

Tulsi

Leaves!

32. Eagle

Keen eyed; Majestic winged
Hovering the blue yonder
Oh! The Eagle
The azure's king

Fearless flight; Instant descend
Striking accuracy of time
Oh! The Eagle

The azure's king

Undaunted spirit; Clear instinct
Raging straight into the storm
Oh! The Eagle
The azure's king

Epitome of royalty; Noble being
That every idiosyncratic wishes to be
Oh! The Eagle
The azure's king!

33. Hornbill

On a sunny day
A young rabbit hopped to the river
Something caught his eye on the way
A yellow glare making him shiver
Looming in he saw a peculiar sight
"Is that a bird flock?!"

With a bill, appealing bright
And feathers, a royal black
It looked down at him
Looking at eyes of wisdomous grim
A fearful respect erupted from within
It must sure have no twin!

A lone hornbill,
In pursuit for a fill...

34. The Majestic Lion

Birds fluttering in all fours
Zebras galloping away from the grass
With a fire in his stride
And authority that electrified
The king's on the amble...

Drums beating, trumpets blowing,
The subjects stomping...
With fear, trembling...
As the royalty takes on its ramble!

The royalty comes from duty
Duty to family, to society...
Kith and kin his greatest strengths
For whom, like the king, you and I should go to great lengths!

Solitude's power crashes before him,
As he leads, with the pride
Leading to win's a different trade,
Than winning alone in a realm...

Maybe, that makes him the king
And not the tyger...

The face of eminence
The majestic Lion!

35. The Scarlet Ibis

Oh why! Oh why! Did I go to the mangrove?
Now my mind is so stuck with a thought I can't shove
Such aesthetic beauty still in my eyes
Oh why! Oh why! Didn't I think twice?

A striking colour have never seen, I swear
Its an Ibis very rare
An all-embracing red scarlet
Like a garment...

Present in a huge flock
I had my eyes on them lock
That's when it happened
The hunter's cruel gun bombarded...

And now my heart bleeds
Like the colour of the birds
In a state of a lost dove
Oh why! Oh why! Did I go to the mangrove?

36. The Venus Fly Trap

The beetle once saw an intriguing organism
A plant so enhanced with mysticism
It had a single leaf with spikes
And is it reddish nectar? He was so in suspicion.

Of course a plant never strikes
He felt nervous as his fear hikes
As he watched, towards it a fly wandered
Flapping his wings with quick swipes...

He held his breath, as it entered
The reddish nectar, click, the plant snapped,
Startling the beetle, it enveloped the fly in a trap!
Scared, to find his way the beetle staggered,

"An eating plant! All insects it does wrap
Run, run away, else the monster will grasp"
Oh, poor beetle! He didn't know,
It was the wondrous Venus Fly Trap!

37. Epitome of Entity

A distant howl in the dead of night,
The moon in its brightest,
Crystal clear and in its fullest
Shining down,
As the leader, makes his presence known!
Standing on the rock
Leading his pack
With authority and friendship
With brotherhood and loyalty

Protecting and Caring
Skimming the other's flaws
With your strengths
Taking the war together
Victory or Failure
Its always an equal share
Not of the same blood, maybe
But in all gladness you shed it for the pals
Pledges to the pack,
The epitome of entity and coalition,
The wolves...

38. The Boastful Bear

Grr...Grr...
No one has fur like mine
Grr...Grr...
Like cotton and wool, cuddly and fine
Grr...Grr...
Seldom beings can be me
Grr...Grr...
Standing on fours and twos
Grr...Grr...
I catch fish from falls deep,
Grr...Grr...
I strike when they leap
Grr...Grr...
You can't find another like me,
Grr...Grr...
Anywhere let it be!

39. Snake

Oh! Slender one
Gracious beauty on the move...
Slithering through fields and branches
Away from the sun.
You complete the jungle
The evil fortress,
Wandering in hisses and silence
With vigour and venom
Your stance is breath taking
Like a magnet,
Almost hypnotizing
No one's friend,
Oh! Ambiguous one...
Oh! Mysterious one...

40. The unfeigned venom

Talk of cunning and deceit
Doing its best, the Jackal
Strolling the forest scheming
Plans to overthrow and deceive
Most steer clear of it
Yet some get entrapped in its clutches
Not knowing of its falsehood.
A predator with less brawn,
Making it all up with the brain.
The rabbit's white soul
Falls prey most of the time
To the jackal's act and role
Due to innocence so sublime.
A traitor that needs more doubt than trust
The jackal's the unfeigned venom of the forest!

41. The monstrous beauty

The cassowary is flightless-yet
Its no less interesting
Some of the largest avian being
Living among thick trees.

Having a crest so priceless
And the brightest blue neck, glistening...
With an elegance so appealing...
A black cluster of feathers, these
Birds do make us on our tracks, freeze!

The lady being the highness
Laying green eggs & belittling the males,
Once laid they go off on their own trails,
Leaving the heirs,
With their pops...

A beauty so rare,
With beauty comes peril and dare...
Well my friend, know this,
This beauty is monstrous!
Monstrous...

42. Sincerely, the forest

Its autumn today,
I will have to watch millions
Of my golden leaves go astray
I try getting used to the clashes
The daggers in my heart,
Yet each time the pain's no less,
Scrutinizing my pillars crashing
My home mates taken down left and right,
The big cats and the deers,
The birds and the bees,
Gashes my soul every other day...
I don't ask much,
Just a little effort,
Maybe one quarter of your 'save nature pledge'
Before all my foliage loses the war to the desert
A little aid to save my family,
My family...
Sincerely,
The forest.

About The Author

Shafika Fathima

Shafika Fathima comes from the traditional state of Tamil Nadu. She was born and brought up in the aesthetic southern part of the state. She began writing while in school. With time the hobby became a passion for her. Though she does write in several genres, she feels more at home with poetry. She loves getting inspired and lets her words twist around the prompts and thoughts that she comes across. You can find more of her work on Instagram in the handle, _lithappens_ . She has always dreamt about writing a book and is very excited about her debut book! She is currently an undergraduate student.

www.ingramcontent.com/pod-product-compliance
Lightning Source LLC
Chambersburg PA
CBHW050805160726
48004CB00002B/707